Writers Kate Turner, with Annie Nichols

Project Designer Sonia Moore

Senior Art Editor Alison Gardner

Jacket Designer Nicola Powling

Jacket Editor Francesca Young

Pre-production Producer Andy Hilliard

Print Producer Stephanie McConnell

Creative Technical Support
Sonia Charbonnier

Photography Will Heap

US Editor Carolyn Doyle

US Managing Editor Lori Hand

Managing Editor Lisa Dyer

Managing Art Editor
Marianne Markham

Art Director Maxine Pedliham

US Publisher Mike Sanders

Publishing Director Mary-Clare Jerram

First American Edition, 2016
Published in the United States by DK Publishing
345 Hudson Street, New York, New York 10014

Copyright © 2016 Dorling Kindersley Limited
DK, a Division of Penguin Random House LLC
15 16 17 18 19 10 9 8 7 6 5 4 3 2 1
001-291546-Jan/2016

A catalog record for this book is available from the
Library of Congress.
ISBN 978-1-4654-5153-8

DK books are available at special discounts when
purchased in bulk for sales promotions, premiums,
fund-raising, or educational use. For details,
contact: DK Publishing Special
Markets, 345 Hudson Street, New York, New York
10014 SpecialSales@dk.com

Printed and bound in China

All images © Dorling Kindersley Limited
For further information see: www.dkimages.com

A WORLD OF IDEAS:
SEE ALL THERE IS TO KNOW

www.dk.com.

ENERGY Bites

High-protein recipes for increased vitality & wellness

CONTENTS

Powders that pack a punch page 50

Superstar nuts page 32

Fiber-filled fruit page 40

PICK A RECIPE

Treat yourself to a power-packed snack with seven savory and eight sweet, simple-to-make superball recipes.

HEMP-COATED
QUINOA CRUNCHERS
Page 30

TROPICAL
IMMUNE BOOSTERS
Page 42

SUPERFOOD
GRANOLA BALLS
Page 52

CARROT & RED BEET
BUCKWHEAT BALLS
Page 24

PEA GREEN
HIGH-PROTEIN MUNCHERS
Page 26

NUT & SEED
NUTRIENT BOOSTERS
Page 28

SWEET POTATO
SPICY BITES
Page 34

BROCCOLI & MACA
POWERHOUSE BALLS
Page 36

KALE-COVERED
COCONUT BLASTS
Page 38

PEANUT BUTTER
& BANANA BALLS
Page 44

APPLE "PIE"
ANTIOXIDANT BITES
Page 46

FRUIT & NUT
BUILD-A-BALLS
Page 48

CRANBERRY & FIG
SPICE BITES
Page 54

RAW CHOCOLATE
INSTANT ENERGY TREATS
Page 56

AVOCADO & BANANA
RECOVERY ICE BITES
Page 58

SO HERE'S WHY THEY'RE **AWESOME** ...

Eating deliciously healthy, all-natural food is becoming a top priority for more and more people, especially if you lead a busy life or have a growing family to feed. We all want tasty meals and snacks that will make us feel amazing and are quick and easy to prepare. That's where Energy Bites come in. All of the recipes in this book are vegetarian, gluten- and dairy-free, energy-packed, and protein-rich; some are "raw," and all of them are free of refined sugars. So what makes these bites so good for you? These recipes are created with health benefits in mind, and each one

should pack a serious nutrient power punch and deliver a host of vitamins, minerals, and phytochemicals (such as antioxidants and anti-inflammatories) that help support and protect the working systems of your body.

The bites are in a ball shape, loaded with goodness, and easy to grab for breakfast, lunch, dinner, or as a tasty treat. They're portable nuggets of intense nutrition and are handy for adding to kids' lunchboxes, taking to the office, enjoying on a picnic, or even simply as a little taste of decadence, knowing that all of the recipes are really good

for you. Every bite is full of "superfood" ingredients, so you can expect a completely natural health boost and an awesome sense of well-being from these vitality-packed goodies. You can't get much better than that.

Mix and match

The 15 recipes in this book are all fabulous in their own right, but feel free to experiment with your favorite flavors. The basic "Energy Bite formula" is given on page 16, and over the next few pages there are plenty of ideas for ingredients to incorporate into your own creations. Whether you're looking for a pre-workout stamina boost, a muscle-building protein hit, support for your immune system, or even a cool iced treat to help you rehydrate, there's an Energy Bite for you.

Energizing broccoli & maca

Protein-packed kale & coconut

Guilt-free raw chocolate

Nutritious nut & seed

Detoxifying beets

" *Make mine a* **cranberry & fig** *to go, please!* "

1 Lentils A great source of plant protein, lentils are also high in fiber, magnesium, potassium, and folate (vitamin B9).

2 Buckwheat Gluten-free buckwheat has high amounts of vitamins, minerals, and fiber, and keeps the body fueled with slow-release energy.

3 Quinoa Containing all the essential amino acids that our bodies need, quinoa is loaded with manganese, magnesium, and phosphorus, vital for well-being.

4 Oats One of the best sources of soluble fiber, oats help to lower cholesterol and keep you feeling energized for hours.

5 Beans High in protein, when combined with a grain, such as brown rice, beans provide a complete plant-protein source equivalent to meat.

6 Sesame seeds Full of vitamins, minerals, and phytosterols that support the immune system, sesame seeds also help regulate

The **20 ingredients** featured below and on the following pages are the most important components of Energy Bite recipes—they are all unbelievably good for you and pack a **serious superfood punch!** For the best possible results, buy (or, better still, grow) **organic ingredients** whenever possible.

blood cholesterol and may even help fight cancer.

7 Chia seeds These tiny seeds contain high levels of omega-3 fatty acids and have five times more calcium than milk. They are rich in antioxidants, anti-inflammatories, and energy-enhancing fiber.

8 Hemp seeds This source of vegetarian protein helps to regulate energy levels. Hemp seeds are also packed with zinc, magnesium, and calcium, and are a powerful anti-inflammatory.

9 Almonds Loaded with more vitamin E than any other nut, plus bone-friendly calcium,

versatile almonds can be slivered, ground, left whole, and even made into milk.

10 Walnuts Packing a massive protein punch, walnuts are particularly high in cholesterol-lowering compounds, as well as the stress-busting hormone melatonin.

"These ingredients are crammed with goodness!"

11 Cacao Chocolate in its most natural form. Packed with antioxidants and vitamins, it is said to enhance motivation and feelings of pleasure.

12 Coconut oil With potent antibacterial, antifungal, and antimicrobial properties, coconut oil is also the richest natural source of lauric acid, which is said to boost immunity and fight disease.

13 Blueberries Filled with antioxidants, fiber, vitamin C, and cancer-fighting compounds, blueberries are said to be good for the heart, and even to help improve eyesight and memory.

14 Goji berries Containing more beta-carotene than any other plant, goji berries also have more iron, ounce for ounce, than beef.

15 Avocado Full of antioxidants, avocados are also high in healthy fats, fiber, potassium, vitamin E, and magnesium. They are amazing for the skin.

16 Kale
This leafy green vegetable is a fantastic source of antioxidants, protein, iron, fiber, and calcium.

17 Beets Known to lower blood pressure and thought to be a potent detoxifier, beets also support heart health.

18 Spirulina As well as being 60–70 percent protein, spirulina is loaded with iron, calcium, and vitamins, is great for healthy skin, and supports the nervous system.

19 Eggs High in protein, with 20 amino acids in a easy-to-digest form, eggs provide us with every vitamin except vitamin C.

They are also a great source of the omega-3 fatty acids essential for a healthy heart and nervous system.

20 Broccoli One of the most protein-rich vegetables, broccoli is also packed with vitamins and antioxidants, plus compounds that fight illness, improve reproductive health, and reduce the risk of heart disease.

Nuts & seeds

Brazil nuts A fantastic source of monounsaturated fatty acids and selenium, Brazil nuts are great for the hair and skin.

Cashews An abundant source of essential minerals, such as manganese, potassium, iron, magnesium, and zinc.

Golden flaxseed One of the best plant-based sources of omega-3 fatty acids around, and a great source of B vitamins.

Hazelnuts Incredibly nutritious, hazelnuts have high levels of dietary fiber and folate, an important B vitamin.

Pecans A source of antioxidant ellagic acid, which can help protect the body from disease.

Pistachios A fantastic source of healthy fats, protein, and copper, vital for red blood cell production.

Pumpkin seeds A source of tryptophan, which is converted by the body into the sleep-regulating neurotransmitter serotonin.

Sunflower seeds Packed full of essential amino acids, and a rich source of folic acid.

Fruit & vegetables

Apples Dried or fresh, apples add sweetness to recipes while delivering vitamin C, B vitamins, and fiber.

Apricots An excellent source of vitamin A, essential for eye health, and heart-healthy potassium.

Banana Rich in potassium and easy to digest; bananas are great for instant energy.

Carrot Especially high in vitamin A and beta-carotene, one of the most powerful natural antioxidants.

Celery An excellent source of dietary fiber and vitamin K, celery also supports eye health.

Chiles Capsaicin, which gives chiles their heat, has antibacterial and cancer-fighting properties. They are also high in vitamin C.

Coconut Contains lauric acid, which increases levels of "good" HDL cholesterol in the blood.

Edamame (young soybeans) Usually sold shelled and frozen, these are an excellent source of protein, iron, and fiber.

Figs An excellent source of antioxidants, plus chlorogenic acid, which can help to balance blood-sugar levels.

Garlic Contains allicin, which has been found to have antibacterial, antifungal, and antiviral properties.

Ginger Contains the essential oil gingerol, with anti-inflammatory and pain-killing properties. Can also help to reduce nausea.

Mangoes High in amino acids, vitamin A, and the B vitamins, the fruit can be used fresh or dried. It has antioxidant compounds that are thought to protect against cancer.

Onions Rich in chromium, a trace mineral that helps the body regulate insulin production.

Orange/lemon/lime Excellent sources of vitamin C, plus citric acid that can aid digestion.

Peas Rich in phyto-nutrients, vitamin C, and folate. Frozen peas are just as high in vitamins as fresh.

Raisins A great source of sweetness and energy, raisins also have several times more fiber than fresh grapes.

Red bell pepper Has concentrated levels of vitamin C, plus vitamin A and the essential B vitamins.

Seaweed Nutrient-dense, low-calorie seaweed is a potent source of iodine, important for thyroid function.

Sweet potato This versatile vegetable is a much richer source of fiber, antioxidants, and vitamins than ordinary potatoes.

Tomato Contains lycopene, a powerful antioxidant that may help to protect against cancer, as well as choline, an important nutrient that helps with sleep, muscle movement, and memory.

Grains & beans

Brown rice Whole grains, such as brown rice, can help reduce the risk of heart disease. Brown rice is also rich in selenium and manganese.

Bulgur wheat Containing iron and the B vitamins, bulgur wheat is a great source of energy, fiber, and protein, though it is not gluten free.

Chickpeas (garbanzo beans) Including high levels of vitamin B_6, iron, magnesium, and fiber, these beans, including the flour, are a great vegetarian source of protein.

Yellow split peas Extremely beneficial for health, split peas contain soluble fiber to help lower cholesterol and regulate blood sugar, and cancer-fighting isoflavones.

The Sticky Stuff

Apple cider vinegar An ancient folk remedy, apple cider vinegar has insulin-regulating properties, helping to lower blood-sugar levels.

Coconut milk Nutritious and dairy-free, canned coconut milk offers all the health benefits of coconut while adding a rich flavor to recipes.

Maple syrup Pure maple syrup has a unique sweet flavor, contains immune-boosting zinc, and also has antioxidant properties.

Miso paste Made from fermented soybeans, Japanese miso paste is high in complete proteins that contain all the body's essential amino acids.

Olive oil Rich in monounsaturated fatty acids, renowned for their cholesterol-balancing properties.

Rice syrup An alternative to refined sugar, rice syrup offers many of the B vitamins and minerals that are found in brown rice.

Tahini (crushed sesame seeds) This creamy paste is a fantastic source of calcium, potassium, lecithin, magnesium, and iron.

Tamari A wheat-free soy sauce, tamari provides niacin (vitamin B3), manganese, and the mood-enhancing amino acid tryptophan.

Raw honey With antibacterial, antifungal, and antiviral properties, raw honey is also a powerful natural antioxidant and healer.

Vegetable broth Used in the hemp-coated quinoa crunchers recipe on page 30, it is easy to make. Sauté onions in a large saucepan with a little oil, add vegetables, such as celery, garlic, mushrooms, and carrots, and herbs, such as thyme, bay, and rosemary, add plenty of water, and simmer for 40 minutes, then strain and store in the refrigerator for up to a week or freezer for up to three months.

Spices

Allspice Also known as Jamaican pepper, allspice has a warming flavor and anti-inflammatory properties. It contains the essential oil eugenol, which is antiseptic.

Cinnamon Contains the highest antioxidant strength of all natural foods and is also an excellent source of essential minerals.

Cloves High in eugenol, an essential oil with local anesthetic and antiseptic properties.

Cumin These distinctively flavored seeds are an excellent source of health-boosting essential oils.

Garam masala A blend of several spices commonly used in Indian cooking, such as coriander seeds, cumin, cardamom, mustard seeds, fenugreek, and caraway.

Nutmeg Best freshly ground or grated, nutmeg may have antifungal, antidepressant, and antioxidant properties.

Paprika Made by grinding dried capsicum peppers to a powder, paprika can be hot, sweet, or smoky, and it has antibacterial and anti-inflammatory properties.

Turmeric A powerful anti-inflammatory and immune booster, turmeric has been used for centuries in Chinese and Indian medicine.

Herbs

Basil With exceptionally high levels of antioxidant beta-carotene and vitamin A, basil also contains eye-protecting zeaxanthin.

Cilantro A rich source of vitamins K, A, and C, the leaves (and coriander seeds) have antioxidant properties.

Mint The flavor comes from the essential oil menthol, which has pain-killing properties, and it can also aid digestion.

Parsley Rich in antioxidants, parsley is also high in vitamin K, which may help to promote bone health.

Thyme Contains antiseptic thymol and is packed with potassium that can help regulate blood pressure.

The rest

Acai powder Made from dried acai berries, this can boost energy and help support the immune system.

Baobab powder Powdered dried baobab fruit is low in sugar and fat, and rich in vitamin C, calcium, iron, magnesium, and potassium.

Bee pollen Packed with protein, antioxidants, vitamins, and minerals, bee pollen contains nearly all the essential nutrients the body needs.

Lucuma powder The "superfruit" lucuma has been eaten in Peru since 200 AD. Powdered lucuma offers natural sweetness without raising blood sugar, and is also rich in iron.

Maca powder This mineral-rich powder can help to regulate hormones and boost energy, and is even said to improve fertility.

Matcha powder Made from green tea, matcha contains unique, potent antioxidants called catechins, said to have cancer-fighting properties.

Moringa powder Known as the "miracle tree" thanks to its health benefits, moringa is a great source of vitamin A, C, iron, and calcium.

The Energy Bite **FORMULA**

There are literally hundreds of ways to combine ingredients to make the perfect "bite." Here is a simple guide to get you started on creating your own versions using basic foodstuffs. The ingredients you choose—*fruit, nuts and seeds, powders,* plus the *sticky stuff* that binds everything together—will depend on what's in your cupboard and what you want at the time.

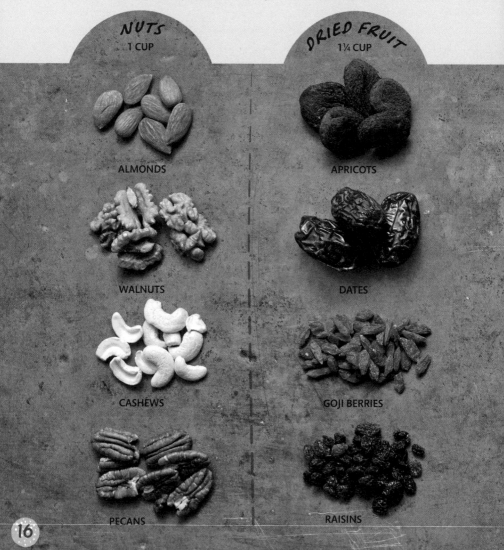

NUTS
1 CUP

DRIED FRUIT
1¼ CUP

ALMONDS

APRICOTS

WALNUTS

DATES

CASHEWS

GOJI BERRIES

PECANS

RAISINS

Simply choose **one ingredient** from **each category** (a combination from the same category is fine, too, as long as you use the proportions given, and omit nuts if allergic) and process in a food processor. **Shape into balls** and roll in your choice of coatings, then place in the refrigerator for 1 hour (if you can wait that long), until firm. Simple.

ta-da!

NUTS ✦ DRIED FRUIT ✦ POWDER ✦ STICKY STUFF ✦ COATING =

POWDERS
1-2 tsp

MACA

ACAI

BAOBAB

SPIRULINA

STICKY STUFF
1 tbsp

TAHINI

COCONUT OIL

RAW HONEY

FRUIT JUICE

COATINGS
Variable

CHIA SEEDS

CACAO

BEE POLLEN

CRUSHED NUTS

17

HOW TO
MAKE NO-BAKES

Other than being incredibly good for you, the best thing about **RAW Energy Bites** is that they are really **EASY** to make.

Make the balls abou

1 1|2 inches

in diameter

1 start with a food processor

Put all the raw ingredients together into the bowl of a food processor.

2 Form a stiff paste

Process the ingredients until they bind together. Depending on the size and power of your processor, you may need to stop it occasionally and push the ingredients down with a spatula before turning it on again.

3 Roll into balls

Divide the mixture into 16 even portions on a tray or plate. Using your hands, roll the portions into round balls. If the mixture is sticky, it will help to have slightly wet hands.

Making by hand

You can also make these bites without a food processor. Typically, you will need to chop up any dried fruit and herbs with a sharp knife, and grind any nuts and seeds using a mortar and pestle. You will also need to mash or puree any cooked vegetables with either a mashing utensil or a handheld blender. You can then combine all the ingredients in a large bowl.

4 Cover in coatings

Spread your choice of coatings evenly on separate plates or trays. Take one of the bites in your hand and roll it gently in the coating. Place on a clean plate.

5 Let them set

Place the bites in the refrigerator for about an hour before eating to help them keep their shape.

6 Store

If you don't want to eat the bites immediately, store them in airtight plastic or glass containers in the refrigerator, where they will last for about a week. They will last for up to a month in the freezer.

HOW TO MAKE **SAVORY BITES**

SAVORY bites are slightly more complicated to make, because you may need to STEAM or ROAST some vegetables, or COOK some onions and garlic, before processing.

Soak *dried beans and lentils overnight*

Some of the recipes require soaking dried beans and lentils. Simply place them in a jar, cover with cold water three times their depth, and let soak overnight. Drain and rinse under cold running water.

Boil *grains and dried beans*

Soaked dried beans and lentils need cooking, as do grains. Put beans or grains into a saucepan and cover with cold water. Bring to a boil, cover, and simmer until soft.

Steam *or roast vegetables*

Some of the recipes require steamed vegetables. Place them in a steamer pan and steam for the required time until soft. Others require roasting. Put the vegetables into a baking pan, cover with aluminum foil, and roast until soft. The aim of both methods is to cook the vegetables until completely done.

Pan-Fry
vegetables & spices

Most recipes will call for some onion, garlic, and spices to be cooked until soft and translucent. Use a small skillet over medium heat with some coconut oil.

Season

Salt, black pepper, and any herbs are added after you've processed the main ingredients in a food processor. Use sea salt and freshly ground black pepper for the recipes.

Dividing up the mixture

Savory mixtures are often sticky, so you may find it easier to use a teaspoon to divide the mixture. Place 16 equal heaping spoonfuls on a plate or lined baking sheet, top each one with any leftover mixture, and then use your hands to roll into balls. It will help to have slightly wet hands as you roll them.

Bake or pan-fry?

Some of the recipes can be baked in the oven or pan-fried in coconut oil. So, although there are only 15 recipes in the book, you'll end up with plenty of ways to make your bites, all with a great, different taste.

Cool

Let the balls cool slightly and harden on a wire rack before storing them (see page 19).

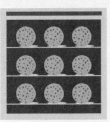

"and now, **15** DELICIOUS, superhealthy RECIPES for YOU!"

look for
NUT-free
RECIPES

CARROT & RED BEET
BUCKWHEAT BALLS

*Includes **BUCKWHEAT**—an easy-to-digest fruit seed that is **GLUTEN FREE!***

Ingredients

MAKES 16

¼ cup dried cannellini or white lima beans, soaked overnight (about ⅔ cup when cooked)

⅔ cup buckwheat groats

2 raw beets, unpeeled and coarsely chopped (about 1 cup prepared)

3 carrots, unpeeled and coarsely chopped (about 1⅓ cups prepared)

15 Brazil nuts

2 tbsp hulled hemp seeds

4 garlic cloves, crushed

2 tbsp coconut oil

2 tbsp apple cider vinegar

¼ cup chopped parsley

Method

1 Drain the soaked cannellini beans and rinse under cold running water. Bring 1¼ cups water to a boil in a saucepan and add the beans. Cover, return to a boil, and simmer for 20 minutes, until soft. Drain and set aside. If using lima beans, simmer for 40–60 minutes, until soft.

2 Preheat the oven to 400°F.

3 Rinse the buckwheat under cold running water. Bring 1¼ cups water to a boil in a saucepan and add the buckwheat. Cover and simmer for 10 minutes, until soft but not soggy. Drain and set aside.

4 Steam the beets and carrots for 15–20 minutes, until soft.

5 Put the remaining ingredients (except the parsley) into a food processor and puree. Scrape the mixture into a bowl.

6 Divide it into two. Place half back in the food processor with the carrots and puree. Scrape into a clean bowl and set aside.

7 Put the beets and remaining mixture in the food processor and puree. Scrape into another bowl and set aside.

8 Divide the buckwheat and parsley between the bowls, season with salt and pepper to taste, and stir gently until combined.

9 Line a large baking sheet with parchment paper. Divide the mixture into 16 even portions and roll into balls.

10 Bake for 20 minutes. Let cool for a few minutes on a wire rack before serving hot.

For one ball: Calories 81 · Fat 4.2g · Carbohydrates 8.8g · Sugar 1.8g
Sodium 11mg · Fiber 1.7g · Protein 2.3g · Cholesterol 0mg

This is a sticky mixture, so it can help to have slightly wet hands when rolling.

Supertip

Making by hand

The recipe works just as well by finely chopping and mashing the ingredients. Simply replace the nuts with 3 tbsp of store-bought nut butter.

PEA GREEN
HIGH-PROTEIN MUNCHERS

*Edamame's high protein and **AMINO ACIDS** make it great for vegetarians.*

Ingredients

MAKES 16

1¼ cups fresh or frozen shelled peas

1¼ cups frozen shelled edamame (young soybeans)

½ cup rolled oats

3 tbsp peanut, almond, or cashew butter

3 tbsp hulled hemp seeds

2 tsp matcha powder (optional)

juice of 1 lemon

2–3 tbsp coconut oil

Method

1 Blanch the peas and beans in a saucepan of lightly salted boiling water for about 4 minutes until just tender, then drain and let cool.

2 When cooled a little but still warm, put the drained peas and edamame into the bowl of a food processor. Add the oats, nut butter, hemp seeds, and matcha powder (if using).

3 Squeeze in the juice of half a lemon and puree until it holds together when squeezed with your fingers. Transfer to a bowl and season with salt, pepper, and more lemon juice to taste.

4 Divide the mixture into 16 even portions and roll into balls.

5 Heat a large skillet over high heat, add 1½ tablespoons of coconut oil, and cook the balls until lightly golden all over. (You may need to do this in batches, adding more oil to the pan halfway through.)

Alternatives

You can also eat these balls raw. Refrigerate for 1 hour before serving.

Alternatively, bake them on a lightly greased baking sheet in the oven at 350°F for 20–25 minutes or until lightly golden and heated through.

For one ball: Calories 114 · Fat 7.7g · Carbohydrates 5.2g · Sugar 1.5g
Sodium 33mg · Fiber 2g · Protein 6.2g · Cholesterol 0mg

NUT & SEED
NUTRIENT BOOSTERS

*A **HIGH-FIBER** snack to maintain your energy and **BLOOD SUGAR** levels.*

Ingredients

MAKES 16

⅓ cup dried chickpeas (garbanzo beans), soaked overnight (1 cup cooked)

2½ tbsp brown rice (about ½ cup cooked)

½ cup red lentils (about 1 cup cooked)

¾ cup chopped broccoli

½ red bell pepper, seeded and finely chopped

1 stalk celery, finely chopped

3 tbsp each shelled pumpkin seeds and sunflower seeds

1 tsp fresh thyme leaves

¾ cup raw cashews

⅓ cup raw whole almonds

½ tsp tamari

1 tsp red miso paste

to coat: sesame or chia seeds (optional)

Method

1 Drain the soaked chickpeas and rinse under cold water. Bring 1¼ cups salted water to a boil and add the chickpeas. Return to a boil, cover, and simmer for 1 hour, until the chickpeas are soft but not soggy; they should have some "bite." Drain and set aside.

2 Bring the rice to a boil in salted water, then simmer for 30 minutes, or according to package directions, until soft. Drain and set aside.

3 Rinse the lentils under cold water. Bring 1¼ cups salted water to a boil in a saucepan and add the lentils. Return to a boil, cover, and simmer for 10 minutes, until the lentils are soft but not soggy. Drain and set aside.

4 Combine the rice, lentils, raw broccoli, raw bell pepper, raw celery, seeds, and thyme in a large mixing bowl.

5 Put the chickpeas, nuts, tamari, and miso into a food processor and process to a coarse paste. (You don't want a puree, so don't overdo it.) Add the mixture to the large bowl and combine well. Season with sea salt and freshly ground black pepper.

6 Preheat the oven to 400°F. Line a large baking sheet with parchment paper. Divide the mixture into 16 even portions and roll into balls. If desired, roll the balls in sesame seeds or chia seeds to coat them. Place on the baking sheet.

7 Bake in the preheated oven for 20 minutes, until golden brown. Remove and let cool on a wire rack for a few minutes before serving hot. Alternatively, bake, let cool, and serve cold.

For one ball: Calories 111 · Fat 6.2g · Carbohydrates 9.3g · Sugar 1.2g
Sodium 26mg · Fiber 1.8g · Protein 5.1g · Cholesterol 0mg

Making by hand

Replace the almonds and cashews with ¼ cup store-bought almond butter and ⅓ cup cashew butter. You will need to mash the chickpeas well by hand and combine with the nut butters, tamari, and miso. Add the mixture to the rice-and-vegetable mixture and stir it all together. Season with salt and pepper.

HEMP-COATED
QUINOA CRUNCHERS

Contains FIVE of the top SUPERFOODS for health and vitality.

Ingredients

MAKES 16

2-3 raw beets (about 7 oz)

juice of 1 lemon

½ cup quinoa

1¼ cups vegetable broth

½-1 red chile, seeded
and finely chopped

1 garlic clove, crushed

1 tbsp chopped parsley

½ cup chopped pecans

2 tsp ground cumin

pinch of smoked paprika

½ cup chickpea (besan) flour

⅔ cup hulled hemp seeds

2-3 tbsp coconut oil,
if frying

Method

1 Preheat the oven to 350°F. Put the whole beets into a baking dish. Cover with aluminum foil and bake for about an hour or until tender when pierced with a small, sharp knife.

2 When cool enough to handle, peel the beets and cut into chunks. Puree in a food processor or mash well with half the lemon juice until pureed. Scrape the puree into a large bowl.

3 Rinse the quinoa in a strainer under cold water, then drain. Bring the broth to a boil in a saucepan and add the quinoa. Return to a boil. Cover, reduce the heat, and simmer for about 20 minutes or until the quinoa is tender and almost all the liquid has been absorbed. Put into a strainer to drain and cool.

4 Scrape the cooled quinoa into the bowl of pureed beets. Add the chile, garlic, and parsley, then stir in the pecans, cumin, smoked paprika, and flour. Season with salt, pepper, and lemon juice to taste.

5 Shape the mixture into 16 even balls. Spread out the hemp seeds on a large, flat surface and roll the balls evenly in them.

6 Heat a large skillet over high heat, add about 1½ tablespoons of coconut oil, and cook the balls until lightly golden all over. (You may need to do this in batches, adding more oil to the pan halfway through.)

Alternative

Bake the balls on a lightly greased baking sheet in the oven at 350°F for 20-25 minutes.

For one ball: Calories 80 · **Fat** 4.8g · **Carbohydrates** 6.2g · **Sugar** 1.5g
Sodium 32mg · **Fiber** 1g · **Protein** 3.4g · **Cholesterol** 0mg

SuperSTAR NUTS

Cashew

High in magnesium, which is vital for healthy bones, cashews are also rich in iron, phosphorus, zinc, copper, and manganese. They help support memory and concentration.

Pistachio

Packed with 6 grams of protein per ounce, pistachios are little green sticks of dynamite. Full of antioxidants, they also support eye health and regulate hormones.

Brazil nut

Rich in selenium, a powerful antioxidant, and in minerals that support thyroid function and the immune system, Brazil nuts are also a good source of vitamin E.

Pecan

These nuts can help regulate cholesterol levels and support heart health, because they contain plant sterols and oleic acid, an important monounsaturated fatty acid.

Cashew

Pistachio

Brazil nut

Pecan

SWEET POTATO
SPICY BITES

Turmeric, chile, and cumin help FIRE UP your METABOLISM.

Ingredients

MAKES 16

½ cup dried chickpeas (garbanzo beans), soaked overnight (about 1¼ cups cooked)

1 sweet potato, unpeeled, cut into chunks

1 tbsp coconut oil

½ red onion, finely chopped

2 garlic cloves, crushed

1 tsp ground turmeric

1 tsp ground cumin

1½ tsp finely chopped red chile

juice of ½ lemon

2 tbsp tahini

¾ cup coarsely chopped fresh cilantro

Method

1 Drain the soaked chickpeas and rinse under cold water. Put 2 cups of water into a saucepan, bring to a boil, and add the chickpeas. Cover, return to a boil, and simmer for about 1 hour, until soft.

2 Steam the chunks of sweet potato for 15 minutes, until soft.

3 Meanwhile, heat the oil in a skillet and gently cook the onion and garlic until soft. Add the turmeric, cumin, and chile, and cook for an additional 2 minutes.

4 Preheat the oven to 400°F.

5 Put the chickpeas, sweet potato, lemon juice, tahini, and cilantro in a food processor and process for about 10 seconds to a coarse mixture; do not overprocess.

6 Transfer the contents to a large mixing bowl and add the onion mixture. Season with salt and pepper to taste. Stir well.

7 Divide the mixture into 16 even portions and roll into balls with your hands. Place them on a baking sheet lined with parchment paper and bake in the preheated oven for 20 minutes.

8 Remove and let cool on a wire rack for a few minutes until firm before serving hot. Alternatively, bake, let cool, and serve cold.

For one ball: Calories 60 · Fat 3.3g · Carbohydrates 5.9g · Sugar 1.3g
Sodium 9mg · **Fiber** 1.7g · **Protein** 2.2g · **Cholesterol** 0mg

This is a **NUT-free** RECIPE

Making by hand

This recipe is just as good made with a hand blender or a little elbow grease. You will need to mash the sweet potato and chickpeas really well before adding the lemon juice, tahini, and coarsely chopped cilantro.

BROCCOLI & MACA
POWERHOUSE BALLS

Packed with C and B vitamins to BOOST YOUR IMMUNITY and energy.

Ingredients

MAKES 16

⅓ cup shelled sunflower seeds

¾ cup hazelnuts

2¼ cups chopped broccoli

½ small onion, finely chopped

2 garlic cloves, crushed

3 tbsp coconut oil, plus extra if frying

2 tbsp tahini

1 tbsp maca powder

¼ tsp ground nutmeg

Method

1 Put the sunflower seeds into the bowl of a food processor and process until they resemble bread crumbs. Add the remaining ingredients and process the mixture to a paste.

2 Transfer the mixture to a bowl and season with salt and pepper to taste.

3 Divide into 16 even portions and roll into balls. Refrigerate for 1 hour before eating raw.

Alternatives

You can also eat these balls hot. Heat a large skillet over high heat, add about 1½ tablespoons of coconut oil, and cook the balls until lightly golden all over. (You may need to do this in batches, adding more oil to the pan halfway through.)

Alternatively, bake them on a lightly greased baking sheet in the oven at 350°F for 20–25 minutes or until lightly golden and heated through.

For one ball: Calories 107 · Fat 9.8g · Carbohydrates 2g · Sugar 1g
Sodium 3mg · Fiber 1.9g · Protein 2.9g · Cholesterol 0mg

EAT RAW

Supertip

Make these tasty balls in advance and keep them in the freezer—just defrost before eating.

KALE-COVERED
COCONUT BLASTS

Full of **PROTEIN-RICH EGG** *to keep you full longer.*

Ingredients

MAKES 18

1 tbsp coconut oil, plus extra for frying

½ onion, finely chopped

½–1 green chile, seeded and finely chopped

½ tsp ground turmeric

1½ tsp garam masala

pinch of cinnamon

pinch of ground cloves

1¾ cups canned coconut milk

¾ cup unsweetened dried coconut

½ cup dried green lentils

juice of 1–2 limes, to taste

3 hard-boiled eggs, chopped

2 tbsp chopped fresh cilantro

FOR THE COATING

¼ cup buckwheat flour

2 eggs

large handful of trimmed kale, finely shredded

⅓ cup shelled pumpkin seeds, chopped

Method

1 Heat the coconut oil in a small saucepan, add the chopped onion and chile, and cook gently for about 5 minutes, without browning. Add the spices and cook for an additional few minutes.

2 Stir in the coconut milk, add the dried coconut, and bring to a boil. Stir in the lentils, reduce the heat, and simmer, stirring occasionally, for 20–25 minutes or until the lentils are tender and the liquid has thickened.

3 Remove from the heat and let stand until warm. Put the mixture into the bowl of a food processor and process to a coarse paste. Scrape the mixture into a bowl, and season with salt, pepper, and lime juice to taste. Fold in the chopped hard-boiled eggs and cilantro.

4 Shape the mixture into 18 even balls and set aside.

5 Spread out the flour onto a plate and season with salt and pepper. Lightly beat the eggs in a bowl. Mix the shredded kale and pumpkin seeds together on a large rimmed baking sheet.

6 Roll each ball evenly in the flour, then the egg, shaking off any excess, and finally coat evenly in the kale and pumpkin seeds.

7 Pan-fry the balls, in batches if necessary, until lightly golden all over and heated through. Be careful when you add the balls to the hot oil, because the kale will make it splatter. Serve with lime wedges, if desired.

For one ball: Calories 88 · Fat 5g · Carbohydrates 7g · Sugar 1.7g
Sodium 48mg · Fiber 1.7g · Protein 4.5g · Cholesterol 53mg

This is a
NUT-free
RECIPE

Lime wedges
TO SERVE
(optional)

Fiber-filled FRUIT

Figs

Sweet and crunchy, figs are an excellent source of readily
available energy and promote healthy digestion. They are also
rich in minerals, including calcium, which supports bone health,
and contain high levels of vitamins A, E, and K that contribute
to general well-being.

Cranberries

These bright red berries are particularly well known for helping
the urinary system and keeping infections at bay. They also provide
a quick energy boost and are rich in anti-inflammatories.

Dates

As well as tasting deliciously sweet and creamy, dates fortify the
immune system and regulate circulation, with their high levels
of iron and copper supporting the production of red blood
cells. Their slowly released sugars keep energy levels steady.

Apricots

Sweet and sticky, dried apricots boost energy levels. They contain
three times more potassium than bananas, helping to protect
against high blood pressure and promoting a healthy heart.

TROPICAL
IMMUNE BOOSTERS

Anti-inflammatory TURMERIC can help protect against colds and flu.

Ingredients

MAKES 16

1 cup dried mango

¼ cup goji berries

1 cup cashews

¾ cup plus 2 tbsp unsweetened dried coconut, plus extra to coat

1¼ tsp ground turmeric

1 tbsp baobab fruit powder

1 tsp rose-hip powder

1 lime, juice and zest

2–4 tbsp cold filtered water

Method

1 Put all the ingredients except the filtered water into a food processor and pulse until finely chopped.

2 With the motor running, add the water a little at a time until the mixture starts to come together, forming a loose ball.

3 Divide into 16 even portions and roll into balls.

4 Sprinkle a layer of dried coconut on a separate plate and gently roll the balls in it to coat.

5 Place in the refrigerator for 1 hour or freeze for 20 minutes, until firm, before eating. Although best served chilled, you can put the balls into a lunchbox and eat later in the day.

Making by hand

Finely chop the mango (soak your mango in cold water for 5 minutes to soften, if necessary), substitute store-bought cashew butter for the cashews, and mix in the turmeric, baobab and rose-hip powders, and lime juice.

For one ball: Calories 55 · Fat 2.4g · Carbohydrates 8.3g · Sugar 5.9g
Sodium 10mg · **Fiber** 2.1g · **Protein** 0.6g · **Cholesterol** 0mg

PEANUT BUTTER
& BANANA BALLS

Includes **MORINGA POWDER**—*a nutrient-dense leaf with a spinachy flavor.*

Ingredients

MAKES 16

½ cup unsalted crunchy peanut butter

1 small ripe banana

6 pitted dates

3 tbsp ground flaxseed

2 tbsp chia seeds

3½ tbsp almond meal

2 tsp moringa powder, to taste

to coat: hulled hemp seeds

Method

1 Put all the ingredients into a food processor and pulse until the mixture starts to come together, forming a loose ball.

2 Divide into 16 even portions and roll into balls.

3 Sprinkle a layer of hemp seeds on a separate plate and gently roll the balls in it to coat.

4 Place in the refrigerator for 1 hour or in the freezer for 20 minutes, until firm, before eating. Best served chilled.

Making by hand

Simply mash the banana with a fork, finely chop the dates, and combine all the ingredients in a large bowl.

For one ball: Calories 96 · Fat 6g · Carbohydrates 8.3g · Sugar 6.3g
Sodium 22mg · Fiber 2.2g · Protein 3.1g · Cholesterol 0mg

EAT RAW

APPLE "PIE"
ANTIOXIDANT BITES

Includes LUCUMA powder for sweetness with a LOW GLYCEMIC index.

Ingredients

MAKES 16

2 cups dried apples

¾ cup pecans

½ cup rolled oats

2 tbsp maple syrup, or raw honey

1 tbsp lucuma powder

1 tsp cinnamon

½ tsp ground nutmeg

¼ tsp ground cloves

2–4 tbsp filtered water

to coat: powdered raspberry (optional)

Method

1 Put all the ingredients except the filtered water into a food processor and pulse until finely chopped.

2 With the motor running, add the water a little at a time until the mixture starts to come together, forming a loose ball.

3 Divide into 16 even portions and roll into balls.

4 Sprinkle a layer of raspberry powder on a separate plate and gently roll the balls in it to coat, if desired.

5 Place in the refrigerator for 1 hour or in the freezer for 20 minutes, until firm, before eating. Best served chilled.

For one ball: Calories 85 · Fat 4.1g · Carbohydrates 11.6g · Sugar 9.6g
Sodium 2mg · Fiber 2.2g · Protein 1.1g · Cholesterol 0mg

EAT RAW

Making by hand

Finely chop the apple (soak your apple in cold water for 5 minutes to soften, if necessary), substitute store-bought pecan butter for the pecans, and mix in the oats, syrup, and spices.

FRUIT & NUT
BUILD-A-BALLS

Coated in **NUTRITIOUS TOPPINGS,** *these make a healthy sweet snack.*

Ingredients

MAKES 16

¾ cup plus 2 tbsp raisins

1 cup pitted dates or unsulfured dried apricots

1 cup walnuts

1–2 tsp spirulina powder, to taste

to coat: shelled hemp seeds, cacao powder, unsweetened dried coconut, strawberry powder, and finely chopped pistachio nuts (optional)

Method

1 Put all the ingredients into a food processor and process until combined.

2 Divide the mixture into 16 even portions and roll into balls with your hands.

3 On separate plates, sprinkle a layer of each of the coatings. Gently roll each ball into one of the coatings.

4 Place the balls in the refrigerator for 1 hour, until firm, before eating. Best served chilled.

 ### Making by hand

Use ½ cup of store-bought nut butter instead of walnuts, and chop or mash your choice of dried fruit as finely as possible. Put all the ingredients into a mixing bowl, mix, roll, and coat, and—presto—a more textured build-a-ball.

For one ball: Calories 86 · Fat 5.4g · Carbohydrates 8.2g · Sugar 8.1g
Sodium 8mg · Fiber 0.9g · Protein 1.8g · Cholesterol 0mg

EAT RAW

POWDERS *that* PACK a PUNCH

Maca

A root that belongs to the radish family, maca was used by Inca warriors to increase strength and stamina before battle. It also regulates hormones and is great for the skin.

Matcha

The finely ground powder of green tea, matcha is high in antioxidants, fortifies the immune system, increases energy, boosts memory and concentration, and detoxes the body.

Acai

The powder of the acai berry has ten times more antioxidants than grapes and, in addition to its ability to fight free radicals (which cause cellular breakdown and aging), it boosts energy and promotes healthy digestion.

Baobab

Derived from the African fruit, this fatigue-fighting powder has six times more vitamin C than oranges, six times more potassium than bananas, and twice as much calcium as milk.

Maca

Matcha

Acai

Baobab

SUPERFOOD
GRANOLA BALLS

Contains AMINO ACIDS that help MUSCLES recover and repair.

Ingredients

MAKES 16

⅔ cup blueberries, fresh or frozen

2½ tbsp maple syrup, 3½ tbp rice syrup, or ¼ cup raw honey

¼ cup coconut oil

1 cup rolled oats

3 tbsp pumpkin seeds

3 tbsp sunflower seeds

5 tsp chia seeds

½ cup slivered almonds

¼ cup almond meal

3 tbsp raisins

¼ cup goji berries

1 tsp cinnamon

1–2 tsp acai powder or baobab powder

Method

1 Put the blueberries into a saucepan with 1 tablespoon of water. Bring to a boil and simmer until the blueberries are soft and tender. Add the maple syrup and coconut oil and heat until well combined.

2 Combine the remaining dry ingredients in a large mixing bowl. Add the blueberry mixture and stir until well combined. The mixture will be sticky.

3 Divide into 16 even portions and roll into balls.

4 Refrigerate for 1 hour before eating raw.

Alternative

You can also bake these balls. Preheat the oven to 350°F. Place the balls on a large baking sheet lined with parchment paper, and bake for about 15 minutes. Let cool, and serve cold.

“ GREAT for pre & post WORKOUT ! ”

For one ball: Calories 125 · Fat 8.5g · Carbohydrates 9.8g · Sugar 4.7g
Sodium 3mg · Fiber 1.9g · Protein 2.9g · Cholesterol 0mg

EAT RAW

CRANBERRY & FIG
SPICE BITES

The B VITAMINS and ZINC in the MACA POWDER help to maintain stamina.

Ingredients

MAKES 16

1 cup whole almonds

1 cup unsweetened dried cranberries

⅔ cup dried figs, stems removed

1 tsp maca powder

½ tsp cinnamon

¼ tsp ground ginger

¼ tsp ground allspice

¼ tsp ground nutmeg

1½ tbsp orange juice

Method

1 Put all the ingredients into a food processor and pulse for about 30 seconds, until the mixture is finely chopped.

2 Divide the mixture into 16 even portions and roll into balls; you may find this easier to do if your hands are wet.

3 Place the balls in the refrigerator for 1 hour before serving.

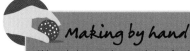

Making by hand

Although these are best made in a food processor, you could also make them by hand. Replace the whole almonds with ½ cup almond butter, chop or mash the dried fruit as finely as possible, and mix in the spices and juice—it's as simple as that.

For one ball: Calories 92 · **Fat** 4.6g · **Carbohydrates** 11g · **Sugar** 10.5g
Sodium 6mg · **Fiber** 1.2g · **Protein** 2g · **Cholesterol** 0mg

EAT RAW

Supertip

These bites are best if they retain some texture and "bite," so don't overdo it when you're blending the ingredients in the food processor. You don't want the mixture to be too soft.

RAW CHOCOLATE
INSTANT ENERGY TREATS

*CACAO delivers **ANTIOXIDANTS**, while bee pollen is a natural **ENERGIZER**.*

Ingredients

MAKES 16

⅛ ripe avocado

½ cup tahini

½ cup raw honey,
⅓ cup maple syrup,
or ½ cup rice syrup

½ cup raw cacao powder

2 tbsp coconut oil

1 tbsp sesame seeds

extra cacao powder, to coat
(optional)

bee pollen granules, to coat
(optional)

Method

1 Peel the avocado. Put all the ingredients, except the sesame seeds, into a food processor and process to a sticky paste. Add the sesame seeds and pulse a few times to combine; the seeds should be whole.

2 Refrigerate the mixture for 1 hour, until firm.

3 Divide the mixture into 16 even portions and roll into balls. If the mixture is too sticky, wet your hands a little.

4 On separate plates, sprinkle a layer of bee pollen granules and some cacao powder, if desired. Gently roll the balls in one or the other. They should be less sticky and easier to roll into a perfect shape.

5 Place the coated balls in the refrigerator for at least another hour before eating. Serve chilled.

This is a
NUT-free
RECIPE

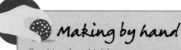

Making by hand

Combine the tahini, honey, cacao powder, and coconut oil (softened) in a small bowl and beat to make a fudgelike paste. Put the avocado into a separate bowl and mash to a lump-free consistency (a mortar and pestle works best). Add the avocado and sesame seeds to the mixture and stir until combined.

For one ball: Calories 89 · Fat 7g · Carbohydrates 5g · Sugar 4.4g
Sodium 2mg · Fiber 1g · Protein 1.7g · Cholesterol 0mg

AVOCADO & BANANA
RECOVERY ICE BITES

with nutrient-loaded chia seeds to **RESTORE ENERGY** *after exercising.*

Ingredients

MAKES 8

8 (2-OZ) POPSICLE MOLDS, CAKE POP MOLDS, OR ROUND ICE-CUBE MOLDS

1¾ cups unsweetened almond or hazelnut milk

2 tbsp cacao nibs

1 tbsp chia seeds

½ ripe avocado

1 small banana

pinch of sea salt

Method

1 Pour the almond or hazelnut milk into a small saucepan and add the cacao nibs. Warm gently, bring to a simmer, then remove from the heat. Let cool slightly, stir in the chia seeds, then let cool completely.

2 Put the avocado and banana into the bowl of a food processor and blend well with a pinch of salt. Add the cooled milk mixture to the bowl and blend again to break up the cacao nibs a little, but not so they are smooth.

3 Using a small plastic funnel or a funnel made from parchment paper, pour the mixture into the round molds. Alternatively, try ice-cube trays. Place in the freezer.

4 When the bites are half-frozen, insert a lollipop stick into each one. Return to the freezer and freeze until hard.

" **Repair muscle & Rehydrate** WITH THIS LOW-CAL **POTASSIUM-PACKED** *snack* "

For one ball: Calories 23 · **Fat** 1.6g · **Carbohydrates** 2g · **Sugar** 1.1g
Sodium 24mg · **Fiber** 1g · **Protein** 0.5g · **Cholesterol** 0mg

FROZEN

GLOSSARY

Amino acids Used in every cell of the body, amino acids are the building blocks for protein. They also aid tissue growth and repair.

Anti-inflammatories Foods with anti-inflammatory properties relieve swelling in the body and can help fight disease.

Antioxidants These help to neutralize free radicals from the environment, which can damage cells in the body and cause premature aging.

B vitamins The B complex is made up of eight vitamins, each with its own function. They help the body unlock the energy in food, and help to form red blood cells.

Calcium Essential for bone and teeth formation and strength, calcium also regulates nerve and muscle function, hormones, and blood pressure.

Copper Helps the body produce the enzymes it needs for iron absorption, helps to form red blood cells, and maintains skin, bone, and nerve formation.

Fiber Can help prevent heart disease, diabetes, weight gain, and some cancers, and can also improve digestive health.

Folate (vitamin B9) Also referred to as folic acid, folate promotes a healthy nervous system, and is especially important for pregnant women to ensure babies have healthy development.

Free radicals Unstable and highly reactive molecules that exist in the environment around us and are said to cause damage to cells, accelerating the aging process.

Glycemic index A number that indicates a food's effect on blood glucose (also called blood sugar) levels. Foods with a lower glycemic index will have less of an effect on blood sugar, whereas foods with a high glycemic index may cause blood sugar to become unstable.

HDL cholesterol High density lipoprotein, also referred to as "good" cholesterol, carries excess cholesterol back to the liver for processing. High HDL levels in the blood reduce the risk of heart disease.

Iron Important for red blood cell function, energy release, and growth. A lack of iron in the blood causes anemia.

Lauric acid Found in coconuts, this is converted in the body into a highly beneficial compound called monolaurin, which has antiviral and antibacterial properties.

Magnesium Important for DNA repair, energy production, heart, and circulation health.

Manganese An antioxidant mineral that is important in bone and ligament formation.

Metabolism The rate at which your body burns energy—or calories—to fuel everyday cell processes and growth.

Monounsaturated fatty acids Improves blood cholesterol levels, which can decrease the risk of heart disease. May also benefit insulin levels and help to control blood sugar.

Omega-3 These essential fatty acids regulate inflammation, promote healthy brain function, and are vital for healthy skin, eyes, and joints.

Phosphorus Important for healthy bones, phosphorus also supports energy production and activates B vitamins in the body.

Phyto-nutrients These plant-based compounds have beneficial effects on the body, working with other essential nutrients to promote good health.

Phytosterols Plant compounds called phytosterols are structurally similar to cholesterol, and can act in the intestine to lower cholesterol absorption and therefore reduce the risk of heart disease.

Potassium Vital for blood pressure regulation, potassium also regulates the balance of hormones in the body and promotes nerve and muscle health.

Selenium An antioxidant mineral that can fight cancer-causing compounds, it is important for reproductive health and fertility.

Vitamin A Also known as retinol, this is important for eye health and vision and for collagen production, which keeps skin healthy. It helps the immune system fight infection.

Vitamin C Supports the immune system and promotes healthy bones, teeth, and gums. Also important in the absorption of iron by the body.

Vitamin E This antioxidant vitamin supports the skin, heart, and circulation, and is important for healthy growth.

Vitamin K Found in green, leafy vegetables, this helps to regulate the blood-sugar balance in the body, heals wounds, and also supports a healthy heart and circulatory system.

Zinc An important mineral that regulates the immune system, aids healing, and supports healthy skin, hair, and muscles.

INDEX

The Authors

Kate Turner has been creating deliciously healthy, happy food for herself and her family for decades. She loves good, honest, tasty meals that make you feel amazing, are packed full of natural energy, and are super quick and easy to prepare! Kate shares her ideas about food, foraging, gardening, and family life on Instagram and her blog Homegrown Kate (homegrownkate. com). Thanks go to her children, Stan, Scarlet, and Tommy, for being the best taste-testing team!

Annie Nichols contributed the recipes on pages 26-7, 30-1, 36-9, and 58-9. Originally a trained chef, Annie is a well-established cookery writer, food columnist, photographer, and food stylist. She can be contacted at www. hotmealsnow.com.

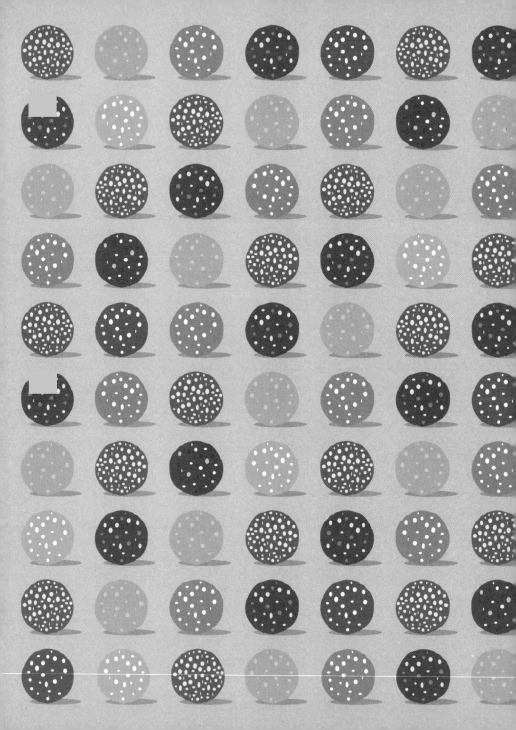